THE SOUND OF GEESE
OVER THE HOUSE

THE SOUND
OF GEESE
OVER
THE
HOUSE

•

poems

June 15 – November 4, 2007

Daniel Abdal-Hayy Moore

The Ecstatic Exchange
2015
Philadelphia

The Sound of Geese Over the House
Copyright © 2015 Daniel Abdal-Hayy Moore

Printed in the United States of America

For quotes any longer than those for critical articles and reviews, contact:
The Ecstatic Exchange,
6470 Morris Park Road, Philadelphia, PA 19151-2403
email: abdalhayy@ecstaticxchange.com
website: www.ecstaticxchange.com

First Edition
ISBN: 978-0-578-16360-4 (paper)
Published by *The Ecstatic Exchange,*
6470 Morris Park Road, Philadelphia, PA 19151-2403

Cover art by the author
Back cover photograph © by Sierra Salin

بس

DEDICATION

To
Shaykh ibn al-Habib
(and the continuation of the Habibiyya)
Shaykh Bawa Muhaiyuddeen,
all shuyukh of instruction and ma'arifa
Baji Tayyaba Khanum
of the unsounded depths

✳

The earth is not bereft
of Light

CONTENTS

...And if a person came to know the bliss within his soul,
he would shed a tear of joy with every breath he took.

He would fly forth from the body that had turned into his cage
on wings of meditation to the Lote-Tree of the Boundary.

And would range the expanses of the Footstool and Throne
where the galaxies appear as but a tiny ring.

He would see the planets' orbits and the mystery of their houses,
and the immensity of the speed at which they pass

And the veil of the Tablet would be lifted from the mystery it enfolds,
and the knowledge it contains would pour forth uncovered...

— Diwan of Shaykh Muhammad ibn al-Habib (*raheemahullah*)

LISTEN CLOSELY

God is here

so where am I

and what good is it?

That bird out there in the dark
staggers its whistles

Now it stopped

My heartbeat is constant

The birds are invisible to me now
but their songs are audible
and each one glorious

Now they stopped

I feel my heart beating
down to the left of me
in my chest

God is here

listen

closely

6/15

THE HEAVENLY KEY

On my account
don't scatter the chickens in the yard
or publish the piano rolls

The earth's flat for easy strolling they say

Rainbows are caught at two ends and
tied to a bush by the roadside

Some travelers glide along the blue arc
some along the red

I've never understood why night should be
black when it falls instead of

gold say or amethyst

Don't move to Schenectady on my account
nor tie the handlebars of the bikes together

We've all got some story to tell
but they collected them yesterday to

melt down for the war effort
which may account for our blank stares
and frequent sobbing

Sometimes I think a goldfish has

a better assessment of the sea

than we do of humanity

God bless the dots on our DNA
and grant us the heavenly key

to save ourselves from infamy

6/18

THE SOUND OF GEESE OVER THE HOUSE

The sound of geese over the house

and in the house the prayer on the Prophet

The sound of geese over the house

and in the house Allah loves you

The mountains are full of light and their
gigantic shadows are eloquent since they're
leaning against the sky and out into space with their
crags and outcrops

No sound can scale in a dimension commensurate with
the pure expanse of it

The sound of geese over the house

puts a dome of life above us and a
sea of life below us and a
world of life all around us

and a shaft of living Light inside us

6/21

STORK ON A CHIMNEY POT

There's a stork on a chimney pot
overlooking the Alps

Flamingos like pink question marks then
a sea of flashes in flight

beneath which a dolphin then another
keep the syntax of waves woven together by their
incessant leaping

so that really world without end
world without end

in one eye and out the other

in the center of the world's forehead

Cyclops in a spin around his own middle

But back home again
the fish are jumpin'

6/22

THE LAST REPAIRMAN FOR OIL LAMPS

The last repairman for oil lamps
sat by his window with folded hands

The last caveman artist with sooty fingers
put his mark on a rock-bulge of bison

The final zeppelin pilot saw his soul
rise into the air and drift past recalling

and so these eyelids close and their lips are
still and the integral knowledges of
exactly how to do what they do are
folded like parchment scrolls around the
spindly fingers of the elves of transition

The Native Americans with their earth symbolism
Aborigines with their dream-time

as the planet turns to give an illusion of sunset and
sunrise

always leveling off into sheep-studded valleys
and scowling mountaintops

and a hut with a chimney and
smoke curling up into the
light of day

6/23

AND JUST AS BRIGHT

A word flies free from is meaning
and lands without warning
on the windshield of the rosiest dawning

A linguistics professor is yawning
at the precise moment of its alighting
and sees its formation and structure

and thinks more of modern sculpture
than of a philology dictionary's rapture
since the word though real seems meaningless

by no fault of its own but some outer stress
that may have traumatized it to make it less
than its essence guarantees by making it

articulate a meaning at the core of its source
that would have allowed the word of course
to come from any language and be roughly

the same meaning cross-culturally not muffling
its slightly skewed reference without utterly
betraying the vocable call of its meaning's central

need to be defined clear as a bell
rung in a mountain village say
where everyone within earshot could without delay

say "*Here's a word that means this or that*"
without equivocation but accommodation a flat
across-the-board agreement it stands for

what it stands for with a kind of light around its flower
as if with a saintly purpose the word
should be ready to serve its place in the herd

of uses in sentences and exclamations
beyond anyone's objections or expectations
but this word lands as if from Mars

like a snowflake tossed from extraterrestrial jars
in another space than that of human –
word four-square and electrically illumined

yet delicately and intellectually unpronounceable
since it has no actual reason to exist at all
except to be part of God's creational mist

that may have a meaning to Himself alone
that we may know in the marrow of our bones
has as much need to be as a centipede

or a wind off the Nile that bends a reed
who sighs indistinctly as it leans its stalk
and utters a wordless word that stops all talk

and is simply and deliciously itself after all
is said and done and so it is
the word lands on the windshield with a kind of fizz

and sizzles here to confound us all
where it appears in this poem though unpronounced
as raw and round as a billiard ball

pounced on by fate to stand as a tall
thing in itself and as pure as love
to be used as form-fittingly as a glove

over thumb and four fingers in usefulness
not an atom more nor an atom less –
Word so pure it stands on its own

the Lord of its domain on a heavenly Throne
landed in this world to enlighten our hearts
out of their rational counterparts

with an *aha!* that goes beyond comprehension
and intimates reality's full dimension

as straightforward as light
and just as bright

6/24

THE EASY LIFE

"The easy life is what I long for" says the
man with cosmoses osmosising inside him

giving birth to stars actually visible in the sky

Our lives are whodunits with every clue leading back
to the Creator Who didn't create us as a

flight of fancy and whose battlefields with
real dead in them are proof of the

utter seriousness of our situation

There's the sound of a city chewing itself to death
and the sound of a prairie waking up and
rubbing the wild wheatfields of its eyes
in the morning dew

And the stars in the sky are God's
furniture no one sits in
with rivers of light that begin somewhere in
deep space and flow through us
in even our simplest and most innocent transactions

dropping one clue after another forward
deciphering one clue after another backward
toward both past and future indiscretions

each action of ours delineating His perfect
dimension as if with a luminous marker
in the very starry sky we've given birth to

in the very air we breathe as it fashions
a fountain in the Unseen
courtyard of His unceasing love

6/25

JUST BEFORE TURNING IN

Just before turning in to sleep
the fly that all day I'd been

pleading with to come to the screen
door so I could let it out to join its

fellows landed on my left hand and
sat quite still even still enough for me

to get up cross the room to the
screen door open it and let it

out into the night and it didn't
fly off my hand en route but seemed to

be saying *"Well I inspected every
corner of your room and literally*

*bugged the hell out of you all day so
now if you'll just get me over there to*

the screen door I'll bid farewell!"

Which it did

6/26

A STRANGE SIDEWAYS WAY

A strange sideways way of showing how
things are

The last swish of a horse's tail as the
full body of the horse disappears around a
bush

or the smoke from a fire but no fire
or nothing for the fire to burn
but still a shadow of a structure burning
flickering against white pavement

Traces of speech long after the speaker's gone
under the earth perhaps or just into
another room but the words have a way of

hanging in the air and form ribbons of a kind of
rainbow light to seem to thread through them

as they sink back into silence

and even silence sinks back into planetary
background noise really only measureable by high-
tech astronomical gauges

since we all talk about God in the most
oblique way to not sunder Him

though prophets are not so constrained and run the
risk of death or punishment for being so

direct and letting no barrier remain between us
and the landscape of strangeness beyond our

usual perceptions though in reality it's Reality and no
landscape or strangeness at all

Larks in trees unseen to the eye but audible

Arrivals and departures making of the
presence of a beloved one an island between two
eternal seas stretching out either side
a sweet island of the Beloved's Presence

A light in a distant room going off
and the person whose words were

suspended in rainbow ribbons
returns to inhabit the
very voice again
that spoke them

6/27

ENCOILED

The lovers encoiled as if in a conch
The Beloved's an echo as if at a beach

The horizon's what joins them

Water and sky aching for an embrace
into each other's domain

The Beloved's a golden bicycle going downhill
The lovers both brakes and lack of brakes

velocity their embrace and liftoff
the lightness of their momentary blur

The lover's a breath that blows the flame into
conflagration

and the Beloved's what fuels the flame and
burns beyond recognition

But the moment of their ignition's their love
made perfectly plain

and the heat they give off
their words of endearment

though only the Beloved remains
and nothing of the lover

Only the Light remains
and nothing of the ash

Only a burning moth remains
become both flight and flame

6/27

ALL OF THEM

All of them were as silent as shale

All of them saw the circus through the eye of a needle

All of them wore spray trousers and waterfall shirts

None of them were missing

One by one they disappeared into the tangly wood

Each leaf of the forest shivered a little
at their arrival

All of them wore shoes of burnished copper

The Queen's letter came too late to stop them

The horses black and blue could be heard
whinnying under the hill

The housetop roofs could be seen from here
a mile away

All of them turned out to be none of them

So none of them were missing

7/5

THE RIDDLE

There's a riddle hanging in the air
whose answer can't be predicted

Everyone knows the answer
but it's as if tattooed inside our skins

Every human being on earth
speaking whatever language knows of it

and a look in the eyes or
an offhand remark may reveal it

It's not even complicated
but it does stretch from one end to
the other of our earthly existence

Sometimes we see it scratched on old stones
or left in a carving among woods untouched
by any knife

I shall pass out of this life
as if on the grease of its runners

Pennants in bright sunlight flap out
its articulation

None of us can do without it
and its answer liberates our souls

It might be easier if each of us were
given only one word of it

Or it might have been a good excuse then
for our confabulation or weariness in
finding out its answer

But we've all been given it complete end to end
and must fill in the blanks with our
breaths

Yet it's not a matter of "must" as
much as a matter of being

And not a matter of being as much as a
matter of not being before True Existence

as if perforated with so many tiny holes
a full spray of spectrum'd light pours through in
a blinding white radiance

And we know from then on the answer
and only then know how the riddle
came about in the first place

and why it was placed in each one of us
and why only the each one of each one of us

is the only one who will answer it

7/6

EVERYTHING'S AN OFFSHOOT

Everything's an offshoot of something else
just as we are offshoots

So a boat on the high seas being tossed by waves
got there by a web of circumstances that
includes the tempest sunset whose
gorgeous glory fills the doomed with joy

Is our job to cut some shoots and
let others prosper?
Not all lead to healthy outcomes
but all are intertwined

A black rose filled with venom
as much as that deep red one filling the
house with death-defying fragrance

Each extension of ours from here to there
interconnectedly resulting from

that event now sliding into obscurity
while another event emerges with its
painted backdrop of sheep-filled valleys
under pellucid skies

One step away or toward somewhere rather than
somewhere else making a perfect
pattern if seen from above perhaps that being

the vantage from which the star shapes and
snowflake designs the circle coils and
black holes of our lives can be
discerned

leading always back (and forward) to a
divine spring rushing over

slick rock beds of wonder

7/6

IN A GLIMPSE

In a glimpse of burst yellow he saw
the end in sight

and from the eclipse turned to the
task at hand

whose watery braid he discerned in the
hands of better horsemen

whose voices called out as one
under the wall

so without warning and without prevarication
he froze to the spot

into which and out of which the whole world
flowed and continues flowing

from sea to shining sea

and now that spot frozen to its wholeness
envelopes the world

by God's design

7/8

ONE SAINT STOOD

One saint stood by the side of the road
and exotic fruits kept falling into his hand
which he gave to passersby

and at the first bite felt elated

Another stood by a lake in a poor town and
fish fell at his feet after flipping through the
air which he handed to young boys and girls

and their families witnessed a glow around
everything for three days after eating their

first fresh fish fry

A third saint sat in the same spot for a
week and night refused to fall on him so that
the people being forced to march themselves into
exile could see their way by daylight along
their endless road

and when night finally fell on them they
felt comforted

I don't know the names and dates and burial
locations of these saints in fact I've

made them all up though they seem to me quite

plausible under the circumstances of pure
sainthood especially after the renewal of
sanctity in this dusty world by the

Prophet *peace be upon him* to whom
rocks sang and all creatures obeyed even the
viper who desisted endangering the villagers

These things aren't difficult for Him Who miraculously
created all this in the first place each web of
leaf or lava laughter or laughing place
and each solemn reply to each sincere

question posed when the saint's eyelids are
deftly raised on the light of each of us

both in our pathetic foibles and in our
noblest grandeur in little things we
barely notice but the

gnats do and the ants are aware of
the saints in us and see in us the earth's
natural radiance in its
heavenly gem-setting making its own

sweet music among the stars

7/9

DO TRIANGLES ON THE HORIZON

Do triangles on the horizon always herald
sailboats or could they be Martians?

If the rain slants upward drawn back
into the sky is everything else also backwards?

If streets and roads tired of always being
trod on got up and trod on us would we
be as patient?

Once you take a different tack the way around
becomes a school for jesters and saints

Ancestry has little bearing but a certain
turned up nose may indicate snootiness

Our anatomies are stuck with us and
we with them from the cradle to the grave but
not beyond

If our graves were dug in the air instead of
the earth would our souls travel any faster?

If the sun's red biliousness gets any more acute
should we take out our parasols
or our sweethearts?

If the earth under us gets any more insubstantial
who should we call on in case of emergency?

If we break the glass and take out the hatchet
then what? Will saving it stop a conflagration?

Words have an interesting way of lighting up
distant corners of the invisible as well as
making the visible disappear

If said correctly *"open sesame"* might also
open up hearts and minds as well as
stuck doors and ancient passageways

Who's to say that turning one's back on the
ways of the world is not the best way of
saving it?

In some cases *"What's the world ever done for us?"*
may be the correct response

Who's to say reducing the problem-makers by one
through detached transcendence or by simply
leaving it alone is not the best medicine?

Theology's always a risky business
though the stock always buys low and
sells high

I've never met a saint who didn't have his or
her feet on the ground but that's all

I love the outer planets they seem so
content in their oracular distances

If someone comes up to us with a knife
behind his back should we take his
smile for granted?

The ants have shown the way for centuries
but we refuse to get down to their level

I've seen the sun rise on a hard slab of ice
and set through leaves of a balmy oasis

Humankind would be better off learning manners
than how to square the hypotenuse of a triangle

A hippopotamus in love is a formidable beast
but a good time to stay out of the water

This train doesn't show any sign of
slowing down so I guess I'll just
jump off

*"God's in His heaven and all's
right with the world"* is a fitting
farewell for the one eyed man in
the country of the blind

and except for that confining
celestial location

it's true however hard it may
sometimes be to accept

7/12

THIS PERFECT SNOWFLAKE

The chance that this perfect snowflake could
fall through space to land on this particular
woolen sleeve and show its symmetry to
me before melting into the nap
must be somewhere in the
billion or two to one range

and I'm saying this during a Philadelphia
heat wave!

So the chance that I should say this
about a particular snowflake in summer
with no snow in sight must be
somewhere in the even more billions to one range
though it's true I suppose that I could say
just about anything about anything though

even that we say only this or that at
any given moment must be also a few
billion billion to one proportion

for we might also stay silent

So it could be argued I suppose that
if there is a particular something taking
place rather than nothing it is the result of
so many fine factors falling into place rather than
none of them falling into place to make a

particular thing happen

and we ourselves with all our special sentience
gestures and thoughts being who we are rather than
rocks or snowflakes falling on someone's arms
or even instead space itself the
flake has to pass through to get here

here one second gone the next

being rather than nothingness...

Ah! God has to finish this poem for me

I've hit a wall

7/14

I REMAINED ASLEEP

I remained asleep for some time
thinking I was awake

Finally I opened my eyes in the dark
and realized I'd still been asleep

Some dream images must have
convinced me I was awake

Now I'm sitting up writing this
though a moment ago I was asleep

What does it take in the end then
to be even more awake?

To awaken from this state and
see it is really asleep?

To go that one step farther
to an eternal state of being awake

and so step out of the land
of the deeply asleep

that thinks in some convinced way
that it's really awake?

Though sleep is a balm and a healing
and a pleasure to be blissfully asleep

I've sat with a saint in this world
who was fully awake

Something mortal in him had been
put permanently to sleep

and without any effort on his part
he seemed totally awake

These are the folk for whom a few
closed-eyed moments are

equal to a night of sleep

For that part that's eternal in
all of us in them is completely awake

The Prophet said he shut his eyes
but his heart was never asleep

There we would find Allah and ourselves
and never regret being awake

and be alive in a moment
that by Allah is never asleep

7/15

THEN ONE DAY HE COULD WRITE NO MORE

Then one day he could write no more

He opened a shop on a street
no one trudged down

selling things no one wanted

He went home to a house
no light lit

and sat at a table no food graced

He lay on a bed no body held
and slept a sleepless sleep no

noise awoke

At dawn no rays entered
his windowless walls

His ticket to Baltimore
held between forefinger and thumb
would take him there

He sat in a seat at a window
and the whole gray world passed by
on its tall bicycles

Then one day he wrote down a word

It brought with it some of its
bosom companions

He had a sentence
then a paragraph

He held onto his pen

He wrote a line
then a stanza

He picked up his pen
and held it above the paper

It hovered there like a cloud
and poured down rain

For a brief moment color came
to his cheeks and his
eyes sparkled

You're reading what he wrote

God knows when he'll write again

7/20

THE SUDDEN STOP AND START

The sudden stop and start of the universe
sometimes causes a kind of cosmic hiccup

Her hand was stirring the batter while studying for her PhD
and the next nanosecond was receiving a Phi Beta Kappa

The engineer putting a chain down to catch on the
edge of the wrecked undersea galleon
suddenly sat in his backyard stunned with a
doubloon in his hand

The Queen of England in her commonplace clothes
was next and with no transition in her
cape and crown and scepter decreed the
end of the war and Britain's immediate
unilateral withdrawal

And what a hiccup! Seas look at themselves
and slide farther out for self assessment before
crashing surfward on shore

Stars turn their twinkle inward and
contemplate both endlessness and isolation
like dots on a screen like sand grains on the Sahara
like thoughts passing through all the
heads of living humankind at once

And yet by God's plan no seam shows no

blip registers and we swim to shore
with no recollection of the

ice canyon that opened up beneath us
or the fiery hell above us

and keep Paradise blowing its tropical
palm trees and its soothingly high-pitched
music in our eyes and ears and its

succulence on our tongues in
deep delight without

interruption from one
moment to the next in

glorious Technicolor
forever

7/22

CRAYON OF LIGHT

I threw a blue crayon of light
out the window across the ocean

to a little village nestled in hills where a
boy who'd just lost whatever most

precious to him could not be lost
and was preparing to carry on with that

loss with a large gaping hole where it once was
and the blue crayon of light flew in a

window that may in fact have been a
bomb-blasted wall and the blue crayon

just happened to land near him who had
seen just about enough of things

flying and landing near him and he
took it in his hands and drew an

outline in the air around himself in
space through which he now

walked into a garden of carpeted wildflowers
radiant in more colors than the rainbow spectrum

demonstrates and he in turn

threw the blue crayon of light through

a window back across the impenetrable
dark to another and another and

another who also drew their
outlines and who also walked free

to where war could no longer
touch them

7/26

THE SLOW ORCHESTRA OF THE WORLD

The slow orchestra of the world comes to life
in the dark dawn

beginning with the birds

The room fan purrs back and forth
pushing away heavy air

Somewhere my soul in all this
sits up and takes notice

Which is more elusive and
runs away faster

the matter world or the spirit world?

My face stops some of the air as it
blasts against my body

Now a bird outside salts the dark
with liquid tweets

I shall die in this position
listening to everything

7/27

FORTUNE COOKIE SURPRISE

One day the fortune cookie writers were
replaced by a host of angels

They took the messages as they streamed down
golden beams and wrote them out on those
little white strips

Some of the messages were so majestic
they broke their cookies and couldn't be
baked in them

Some made their cookies float in the
air like miniature airborne boats on a
mission

But all of them were destined for their
eaters without one exception

The element of chance had been
totally abolished and now the

messages inside on their little white banners
fairly hummed with portent

No more *"You will travel to faraway lands"*
unless they were specific and true
mentioning date and destination and
mode of transportation

No more *"You will be happy"* unless
for a specific reason such as
"Ali Smith of Omaha really loves you" or
"You don't have lung cancer after all"
or *"Your pet parrot Oscar*
will be back by tomorrow morning"

People's children were named and listed
people's affairs revealed people's
business deals unveiled

The cookies were delivered as usual in
giant crates on giant trucks to all the
usual restaurants and grocery stores

Waiters brought two or three out on
little white plates with slices of orange as
usual with the check and the

customers chattered and laughed as usual to the
dry crack of Chinese Fortune Cookies being
opened with the usual nonchalant anticipation

But this time they contained nuclear fuel!

People dropped their shards and rushed out of the
room

Some stared ahead in sweet disbelief as they
popped the broken bits into their mouths

Some tried to put the cookies back together
to reverse the fortune

Everyone's hearts beat a little faster at the clear
recognitions

God's incessant messages delivered
loud and clear as usual

7/29

ENTERING SLEEP

Entering sleep one wonders if we are enough
properly equipped for the

possibility of both unforeseen adventure and
no return

Though we have faith and even pray we'll
wake up on this side the side where this

poem is being written and summer night's
oscillating fan whirrs its motherly waves

But we may not

We may end up way out past the usual edge
where wombats fly and sunsets array their

goldenly garish reds and purples

Oh machinery of dream about to start up your
angelic engines

don't let dark forces interfere with
your more delicate and vulnerable workings

No washing up alone on a sliver of desert island in a
cobalt sea of sharks

No silhouette on ancient castle battlements at
full-tilt anti-rampage above a charging mass like
armored locusts with seas of arrows raining down

Take a lamp and a line?
The way back is the way in?

How many entrances into this lesser sleep do we
get to make before the earthly anchor's cut

and our mortal wedge floats forward past what we
know as both darkness *and* light?

The Face in that darkness and that light
recognizably His

Who fashioned us and draws us toward Him
with every breath

7/30 (67th birthday)

THE LISTENING SPHERES

The story could just as easily be
"The Soldier's Pipe" "The Rabbit's Subterfuge"
"In the Land of Rainbows White Light is King"

or a story about air and who've passed through it
and where they were going or where they

thought they were going!

Such is the reality that no matter where we
start unraveling it or telling it always the

same thing transpires the same various
cutout figures making their delighted speeches
delighted with someone else or with themselves

or just delighted in its rawest form in its
eternal duration with God's Presence as it
showers outward and inward through

everything without exception

So a story could begin at horses' hooves
as they sound their way along cobbles
with the captured princess sidesaddle and her
captor a totally besotted lover who wants to

take her to a garden to sit in her radiance

which she secretly suspects through her resistant
squeals and flaccid protestations

Though this sounds perhaps too classical to
begin with while we might find more

profit in the story of the fish who felt
imprisoned in his ocean and longed instead
for the overhead sky having

eyed it all his life with a kind of
fishy envy its expanse so far outstripping his

watery confines in sheer blue endlessness

Though it's hard to see delight in these
stories which though undeveloped are perhaps more
indicative of fear lust envy dissatisfaction and
passionate desire
as we move along our tracks
tending roses and dealing with
moth infestations

In the middle of each doorway I see
a rectangle to Paradise

In the middle of each water drop the rounded
reflection of our more perfect self

In each sky takeoff the aloft possibility of
permanent transcendence

out of clogged worldliness

And no story however cleverly told can
quite cover it

Though the lion open his mouth to yawn and the
serpent dart in to terrorize him from inside

And the flamingo forget to uncurl its head from
underneath its wing and so be a question mark
posed from then on forever among its
more nonchalant and uninquisitive flock

I hear in every cry the grand declaration of
God's Mercy calling out against itself
to be turned inside-out to silent Grace

So each story while cloaked in tragic garb
for heightened drama

is a peony parading as a black rose
or an ant who's decided it's an attorney

while in true dimensions each mote or
mite of us is afloat in God's elemental current

pulsing from A to B as imperfect swimmers

reciting our heartbeats out loud into the
compassionately listening spheres

7/31

THREE-WORD POEM

A silver horse

8/1

TWO-LINE POEM

I put my head into a cloud

and am gone

8/2

EARTH PLUG

Tonight we have some truly spectacular footage!

Two Russian subs underneath the Arctic
probing for oil

land on the floor of the Atlantic to plant the
Russian flag

when they see a gigantic cork-like object and accidentally
ram it trying to get a

closer look

It pops out and turns out it's the
earth's plug

All the water in the
oceans rushes out and the whole planet

deflates like a big squashy balloon with
water and continents siphoning

out through the opening

and splashing into space!

8/2

A STONE HITS THE GROUND

A stone hits the ground and
wonders how it got there

A house stands on its foundations
welcoming its guests

A gust of wind turns a corner
and thinks itself clever

A river roars from its source
yodeling its course to the sea

Corks and people float on the world
thinking themselves top bananas

Bananas hide in their skins from monkeys
but when found out are cheerfully chomped

A raindrop never wonders why it was sent
but fulfills its duty wherever it lands

A window sits in a wall letting all the
variable light in indiscriminately

Sights from everywhere are here for the viewing
falling upside down on our retinas before being righted

Signs on the other hand are slipped into sights

the way hands are surreptitiously slipped into gloves

The heart reads divine signs with luminous precision
once the crust of the self becomes lucidly transparent

Nothing by itself is of itself alone
but rather everything's an immediate echo of God's call

Every sound in the universe falls into place
Him humming to Himself within everything that is

We are as much notes of that humming as nightingales and cataracts
waterfall crashes or the twitter of wings in the dark

Where have you gone? Why aren't you listening?
Once you hear it loud and clear

you'll disappear forever

And in your place a person not quite a person
but one of God's specifically and particular

spotlit noumena

sitting in the sunlight or sleeping in the dark
where owls fly and trucks change gears as they chug uphill

Where hills rise up a little higher to be
more noticed in the crowd

Where voices intermingle to form

a single oratorio

Where *amen* can be heard with the first
footfall after waking

Where the earth folds up its cloudy blanket
spinning at its leisure

Where a stone falls to the ground
and wonders how it got there

Where this poem waited for the moment to be born
and now opens its eyes and

looks around

8/4

CHILDREN'S JOKES

There once was a cobbler made so many shoes
he had to specialize in centipedes

There once was a flame thought it was hot stuff
when it got to icebergs it just fizzled out

There once was a diva couldn't carry a tune
she got a servant instead to carry it for her

There once was a fly flew into a flue
and having flown into a flue didn't

know what to do

THE INVITATIONS

They gathered from all the known and
unknown corners of the world

without the slightest idea in the world
what it was for

But the way the gold-edged invitations
announced themselves certainly focused their attention

First a procession of children from their
own principalities in elaborate

costumes of mythical figures followed by
caparisoned animals from

their local menageries with a special
emphasis on painted elephants and

entasseled camels

Then a men's drumming corps
followed by a women's a cappella choir

and finally a complete stranger with
unmistakable saintly characteristics

with a silver tray upon which a
silver box with scenes from each recipient's personal

history embossed on the four sides and
lid which when lifted plays

a most identifiably and associationally
personal song to the intended recipient

And when the intended recipient holds the
gold edged invitation somehow a fluttering rainbow

array of rare Amazonian butterflies surrounds it and
outlines him or her as the case may be

shimmering against the air

And after all this and after the gradual
accumulation of dark clouds overhead

so that at the precise moment they
part for a silver shaft of sunlight to fall

straight down on the print emblazoned on it
igniting letters in scorchless flame enough to

be able to read as if by firelight
and to the soft crackle of faraway music

a hush goes out down through the
procession

a holding of collective breath and a
widening of eyes

and the hush extends
throughout the entire population with no

hovel nor exorbitant palatial pile
left out and no age however feeble or infantile

young or old

Everyone anticipates the out-loud reading of
the gold-edged invitation sent to every single

person on earth

to fully participate in the human activity of
enlightenment God's perfectly elementary

sainthood of just being perfectly human
every single moment of our lives between

our own ears between our own two sides and
between all of us as well between the

oceanic seas and their tumultuous waves and
treacherous undercurrents for which we

need each other's most heartfelt assistance
and the hush is suspended in the

air for a moment all over the earth felt
even below the surface of the sea by various

pods of whale and dolphin

And some take the invitation immediately to heart as
the entire visionary procession fades into thin air

while others throw it down in the dirt
and slam the door

and both God and humankind
know which is which in the

light of day or dark of night when
day is done

8/7

NEARLY NO ONE IS NOTHING ENOUGH

Under the window with a banjo
Hafez strums with precision

Roses haven't a chance and
tear themselves from their stems

The street and the house suddenly become
glimmering stars in the galaxy

"The Beloved's over that cloud or
past that floating debris" he sings

"The Path is drenched in the blood
of all who've gone before

Moonlight can't touch their faces
whose shine is even more luminous

Where their human bodies were
is now wide planetary spheres

God's Countenance hovers in the air
but only their hearts know for sure"

The glass in the room
shivers the liquid inside it

The drunkards are slowly returning

to their attitudes of sleep

The room was filled with their raucous cries
and hearts exploded

The ceiling was far too low
for the needs of their souls

But tomorrow is another night
and day another rendezvous

mindful that this poem has barely
taken off without its inhabitants

Nearly no one is nothing enough
before His splendid smile

The echoes resounding in the room
must be coming from somewhere

All we have to do is find out where
and we're there

Ameen at the beginning in the
middle and *Ameen* at the end

How much blood are we willing to lose
for love of the Friend?

8/10

ONE DAY MAGIC REALITY

One day magic reality overtook real reality
so much so that all eggs laid were golden
and you couldn't get a decent omelet or
sunnyside up anywhere

All beans were magic beans
and stalks the sizes of barstools sprang up
everywhere heading into the clouds and the
fearsome clump clump clump of some
drooling giant's always coming near

And everyone was always getting lost in the
forest and coming onto a house made entirely
of gingerbread and bright colored jujubes
and instead of a loving Martha or Magdalena
a small shrill witch in a hood
putting them in an oven and turning on the heat

Dream became reality as well
so everyone could fly but just as quickly
the sky they flew in would be the
old schoolyard with everyone in fox-heads
punching the sparrow-headed undergraduates to death

People who'd never prayed before were
seen on their knees
passion's tears pouring down their cheeks
their carports full of silver Rolls Royces and luxury yachts

now serving as mosques where people gathered
longing for the old life and some
simple hardships they could call their own

The sound of human voices remembering God in
endless repetitions and sincere fervor
slowly grew louder than the whirr of
elves' wings in the air and the famous
flying monkeys of Oz began to
vanish from the skies

Soon the world resembled this one we now see
you and me as humdrum as a

miracle taking place on an unknown
island off the coast of nowhere

or the crack of a real egg into a
frying pan with the usual sad news
playing on the radio on a windowsill

that's as much a magic casement as
ever but also an illumined passage of

light into the room and sweet breezes
after drought

8/12

THE ROUGH TUNDRA OF SLEEP

I'm about to head out across the
rough tundra of sleep

with a small triangular bag of goose feathers
and a glass for capturing the slenderest of

golden rays of either the setting or the
rising sun

which never sleeps even in the cosmic
fiction of its centrality

while her servile planets circle her in her
starry chamber both benevolently

chained as well as keeping their gravitational distance

Various holes await me I know
and the softest of angel breaths whose

whispers I hope to decipher in
tomorrow's daylight

8/13

A GLOW IN A BALL OF ICE

A glow in a ball of ice
a ball of ice in a ball of flame

A ball of flame inside every
molecule of matter

And inside the glow in the
ball of ice a ball of flame

a dancing shadow going on
with every tick of time

between a million populations
and another million

who in the mirror at the
center of the dancing shadow

become four million souls in
shadow dancing with

four million more
in continuous multiplication

who are ourselves of course
in energy and repose

at the center of every

molecule of matter

in a ball of flame inside
a glowing ball of ice

our shadows dancing
as our souls are free

in a tear shed by God's
theophanic Eye

and then by the eyes
in these dancing millions

whose eyes are God's
theophanic eyes

in every molecule of matter
aglow in the center

8/14

AWAKEN *IN* THE SONG

All the known and unknown birds in the world
circle the drunken singer as he circles

round and round

He sets roses on fire and horses of mist
snort outrageously through fog

Earth itself trembles like a snail's back
at his bodily oracular vibrations

Words hammered out at the body shop
down the road

threaded through space
now gleam like diamonds

gradually becomes *suddenly*
perhaps becomes *inevitably*

a hillside of beauties in gossamer gowns
dancing numerically

The singer never quite finishes his song completely
a cow saunters through mooing to be milked

and the milk that issues from its swollen teets
becomes a melodic meditation on the earth's generosity

Who's in fact singing this song as it's sung?
Is it You in the dark there hidden behind the edges!

A flicker of firelight might light up our faces
as we dissolve both body and soul back into night

A glass rim catching morning's first rays
making of them a circular constellation

that holds the drink that puts
all human strife to rest

though only those already peaceful seem
inclined to drink it

The wind full of bubbles
and the glass full of fish

as in a whale's eyes
the whole world disappears

*Where have the birds
that encircled the drunken singer*

gone?

Back to their luminous
perches on the moon?

Now they too are drunk
and sing all night long

to help us in our sleep
awaken

in the song

8/15

ON THE ISLAND OF REGRET

On the Island of Regret there's no
vegetation

Sand everywhere sometimes stationary
sometimes blowing in the air

One is solitary there

Heartbeats skip around like stones

Where is the face that will lighten our load?

Regret isn't even paper boats put out to sea

It's a flame that might have flared up

A speech that might have made listeners
tremble with joy

A boat that pulls out of harbor

But never passes by
the lingering island of regret

in spite of our cries

8/21

NOT A MOMENT CAN BE LOST

Not a moment can be lost in our
meticulous attention to God

His shadow cast against the corrugated glass
before us

The ripple effect of light and dark
through which we can distinguish His turnings

And their diminishment
and their increase

We are not out of earshot nor eyesight
but how could we commonly apprehend

that which has made our apparatus of apprehension?
Though truly by that He is known

But the distant roar of His flood and its
capping His avalanche and its cessation in midair

His heave of billion against billion and
then the utter placidity that extends from

here to there in the ancient aftermath
of the moment right before us

whose characteristics are a near silhouette
going back to Himself Alone

aligned with ourselves alone

are that which warrants such meticulous attention
like a heart ringed around with ruthless pirates

but who sends a virgin of light across
as a bridge to their sweet undefilement

8/21

THERE NEVER IS AN END

There never is an end to things that
we can see

Windows go on and on infinitely once we've
set our sights on what we can
see through them

Flight is similar

But even being stationary can't really be
said to end

Maybe beginnings are the same

There is such a thing as an
origin and destination those strange
valleys where things arise and come to
nothing or into themselves or
out of themselves completely

Somehow behind all that we see
are tremendous shudderings and upheavals
and this little breeze through the
room is the very tiny extended fingertips of them
delicately caressing as a kind of

secret touch

God's giant Throne Room from which
all things transpire

may be either all silence or all sound
but is in any case beyond our
apprehension

But here in this little universe of ours
floods are a song followed by silence

death a silence
followed by song

8/27

THE CURE

The cure for a long story
is a short sentence

For a long speech
a short story

For broken trust
a short speech

For a shady operator
a short trust

8 /28

THE DUTCH WEAR WOODEN SHOES

The Dutch wear wooden shoes
while Amazonian Indians wear none

The Inuit ride sleds across ice
while New Yorkers take subways under streets

Pakistani villagers fret over cobras
while Philadelphia neighborhoods worry about guns

Some monkeys drink water caught in hibiscus flower cups
while some plants have deep water systems

snaking deep below desert sands

The moon comes out and illuminates everyone
while people in their own dungeons create their own

darknesses

Silence befits the wise who see too much
while know-nothing chatterers chatter on and on

Knowledge for some is bewilderment and awe
while for others it's a club to beat others with

Bats navigate caves by sonar bouncing off walls
while we in our drunkenness

refuse to follow directions

Light in Greenland shimmers off surfaces
while enlightened ones' faces shine

all by themselves

8/30

MOUSE STORY

Like a slim finger of breeze the tiny gray mouse
slipped almost unnoticed into the new
long black plastic humane mousetrap

and I saw pink snout sniffing up one
vent and later tiny pink mouse fingers
with teeny-tiny claw-nails curled
just past the plastic's edge

But it's 2AM and too late to take him to the
woods to release him so he'll have to

content himself with the almond he was
after and maybe snooze though I'm a

but worried about Coffee the mouser who
although in her late 20s by cat reckoning

has really come to bat regarding this new
ceiling pattering and almond-stealing

mouse infestation by standing or lying
guard in perfect watchfulness for three days who
might catch mouse scent and start
tampering with the trap though it's from
China and has a metal works inside with hinged door that
definitely keeps the mouse inside

where he or she will just have to abide
till morning

Goodnight mouse!
God bless!

8/31

THE OBSCURITY THAT COVERS

The obscurity that covers most everything
like an antique dealer's blanket over most of this
world certainly the

reality of exactly how things work and
continue working even maimed or nearly
suffocated to death

and most certainly over the unseen things of
this world into over behind and beneath which
great hordes of scholars and thinkers and
crafty explainers have tried to explain

This obscurity like a Shakespearean fog
where we can make out vague outlines and hear
a partial speech or two in a
language we partially understand

This obscurity part and parcel of our mortal
existence on earth and we

cling to like cliff-climbers holding on with
rope hooks and heel clamps and
great windy wide-open spaces
yawn out below us

all of it down to the *oh so* innocent
atoms and molecules without which the

whole thing that is at this moment simply
wouldn't be

This veil without even going into the
various and manifold veils that exist in
mystic terms that can be
passed through by God's Grace in either a

heartbeat's wink or by intensest spiritual labor

No this veil here this filmy separation between
ourselves and our selves and then our
selves and every other self and the real
being of being like a paisley pattern on an

antique dealer's cloth thrown over it all

is truly and simply the way we have to
know the Thrower of it more than
the thrown

on His Throne from which He
throws

and in so doing so many threads come
apart in our hands and somehow singingly

explain themselves to our hearts without all the
intellectual wrangling that might go into more

rational explanations of every single
cosmological thing

9/1

WHAT THEY DID

The fish that blew the bubble
sank the stone

The hand that signed the edict
cut the throat

The fire that cooked the feast
burned the town

The ash that stayed behind
flew the wind

The blue that filled the sky
woke the sea

The life we lead in light
leads to dark

The dark that holds us close
says *"goodnight"*

9/2

TO TORONTO

In anticipation of my trip today to Toronto
the Nile River has risen five inches and its
alligators are floating on its surface
like paper boats with eyes

In anticipation of my journey today to Toronto
little squeaking wheels everywhere in the
world are approaching a sonic harmony
and about to burst into song

In anticipation of seeing new faces in Canada
canaries everywhere are preening their feathers
and in honor of Pavarotti's death yesterday
hitting High C with renewed vigor

In looking forward to crossing the northern border today
my face is taking turns changing color
not just the usual racial hues but also
turquoise topaz tinsel silver and tourmaline

My compass is turning north straight up
and the things in my suitcase are aligning themselves
to look absolutely neutral and innocent like a
boys' choir on a nun's errand in broad daylight

I haven't been to Toronto before so I'm
practicing to say "out" with a hint of
two syllables and to look as

mooselike as possible to blend into the
background

To take no longer to think than it takes
a chrysalis to mature or a
stone to realize it's at the
bottom of a stream

To continue the contemplation of clouds and
inner contours the way a cartographer
caresses inlets and promontories to get
closer to topographical realities on his map
my poems in their little envelopes like
Zippo lighters ready at the strike of a
moment to burst into flame and light up
nearly nothing

Never for a second to face anywhere but
toward the earth's beloved Kaaba with its
delirious pilgrims in the air or on
land in the market place or in the
silence of a tomb

Leaving ourselves in order to find ourselves at the
outer end like looking through a screen from
one vast emptiness into another across
buzzard canyons and grassy prairies
where shadows crossing over make
divine calligraphies from clouds

spelling here as everywhere God's Name in

material as well as immaterial letters

as evanescent as our breaths
but in a script whose wavers of clear black ink

last forever

9/7

ONE TINY TOOTHACHE

One tiny toothache keeps a giant squid
awake

One famous thorn makes an infamous
lion weep

One overturned milk churn burns Chicago
to the ground

A single act of kindness makes the devil
scream in defeat

In the microscopic world giant deeds are
taking place

One metropolis after another there arises and
falls into utter molecular dust

A subatomic king in his microbial ermines is
ground underfoot by an angry mob

We barely notice these things in our fleet subway
subterfuges against human tranquility

zooming ever faster here and there and
nowhere where everywhere begins to

look the same

and we're at last faced by the same face in the
mirror looking back at us

One wingéd horse took the Master of the Ages
to the heavens

One lote tree of filigree materiality veiled him
from God's ineffable radiance

One voice instructed him and the
world has never been the same

Supreme light filters down to each of us
one by one

Nothing is wasted in the Merciful's
generous expenditure

Our eyes are filled with delight or
shaded by grief

One tree shades us forevermore from the
heat of His Grace

I look for His Face everywhere and
you show it in a wink a look a smile

Self-divulgement takes place right in
front of our face

Heart be quiet now! You're about to

run into the street!

Hands and fingers knees and shinbones
toes and feet

The birdsong in the morning in the middle of
the night can almost already be heard

The day will stretch out its luminous path for
us to pass over

His Gaze on us bathes us in His
radiance whether we

know it or not

One nod is all it takes to bring
a symphony to life

I'll go now and lie back down again
next to my wife

9/10

RAMADAN REDUX

1

If we gathered every flower on earth and
held them out in our hands to

strew at the feet of Ramadan as it begins its
moon-clocked journey through all the earths and

heavens known and unknown to humankind
and every precious stone polished or unpolished

to decorate the first steps along the way
and heralding musicians with ethereal instruments and

voices so unearthly sweet our tears would
copiously flow at the first sounded notes

And all the sweetest prayers were intoned
by halo'd sages from every known revelation

it would still not be enough to mark the
gorgeousness of this month ordained by

Allah for fasting in which that overwhelming
high cascade of light our beloved Prophet

received the Qur'an as a dot so dense it
contains the universe and all the wide-swirling

galaxies around it in which God's echoing Voice
can be heard at last clearly in our own

tiny human ears and tattered hearts and
made plain

2

I stumble out of small sleep like a dark
boat lurching from its berth

I stumble from post-dawn sleep like a
baby who thinks it's a grizzly bear

I stumble out like a prop plane falling in
the Adirondacks looking down at treetops

I stumble out like a vaudeville magician
tripping over his tricks

like a young colt just dropped all wet
from his mother into tall grass

Not enough sleep first day of Ramadan

OK maybe I'll have just an hour more

Just a wink or two more of sleep

3

It was a mouth that said hello to
an ear across the lap of a leg

And a nose for it on a chin that
rested its weary load on a fleet foot

that crossed one arm over the other
above a sea of eyes afloat in the

basin of a belly who'd seen better
days among the ribs of caution and a

backbone of all hell let loose in a
rampage of piety whose forehead

swaggered with a two-legged gait
a pony would be proud of cantering off

from a set of lips dry from want but
all smiles from the difficulties of the

road trod lightly by two swift
cheeks in eager competition to be

rosier than the life force that
animates all this amalgamation

into space

4

A little smoke from a chimney in the distance
writes vaporous messages on a slate sky

We plod toward it with grit and determination
one hand in our bag of provision and the

other out in front of us

cutting through suspended veils of dark and light
that hang down from His impeccable Throne

brushing across our faces with their odorous invitation
to follow the perfume of Paradise to its source

My eyes no longer see in front of them
My mind no longer looks behind me

From side to side the world is basically the same
Each step forward approaches dimensional expansion

The valley in the distance is actually all round us
the herbs at our feet are the fires that burn our dross away

Only light in the distant window remains still
while trees rivers roads and scholars whirl like wind

filling the air with uncountable voices
that finally burst into song

5

O Allah
split the skies and shore up the

sweetness that we may lounge awhile
among Your sterner Lights

Those stars we have for eyes when the
shadows of ourselves dwindle

Part the floods that the tips of submerged
conical knowledges might appear above the

water's liquid lips
and show the sky with migrating birds in

spotlit flocks to Your swift refuge

though it's not in the sky alone but also
under our own pulse that Your scriptures turn

and their echoes reverberate in expanding rooms
whose walls are clouds

Oh what is all this yearning day after day
but drops of honey from the spout of

Your Oneness into our spectacularly
various flasks?

I think of wild horses running along the edges
back and forth on a long horizon under

a blazing sky

The drip of the heart magnified
the voice of the heart taking on

Your timber the way yellow light seeps under
a door into a blackened room

6

The circularity of the punctual sapphire
casts radiant spokes on rainbow poles

that demarcate annihilation zones within which
no survivor sings the top note but

instead is sung by it and held there for an
eternal semi-quaver God's own domain

then fills with music and the deaf
would bend to listen to its hallowed song

9/13-22

THE MEADOW

The meadow that stretches each side
of the Truth

with baled hayricks like wigwams in the
twilight under a full moon

and the most extraordinary tiny flowers each
with the face of someone who lived by it
or died by it or both

And a phantom in long skirt and bonnet
harvesting butterflies by picking them
out of the air

and the liquid horse heads that bob up
above the horizon with their
furious red eyes

And an echo that unifies every element
with its reverberating voice each cricket
creaking old dog barking or nightingale
singing

The meadow that stretches each side of the
Truth

in whose atmosphere everyone thrives

It doesn't take much
a deep breath clear eyes and a heart
open and free of anger

Look at the rabbits hopping across it!
their ears longer than night itself
picking up everything ever spoken in its regard

That elusive thing Truth elusive and plain as
day even in daylight

She wears a garment of roses
and around her there's someone to
smell them there's always someone out of
the brimming multitude who's got a
nose for it

It's not a lost commodity only precious
and in need of our care and feeding

She tosses a rose from her rose garment
over the heads of those multitudes
and everyone of them catches it

I see the untruths riding away on volatile blankets
hell for leather

as if on fiery steeds

9/26

LOVE BEAST

for Shaykh Bukhari of Jerusalem

Strike a gong! The love-beast has
returned with his

pelt of conquests around his waist
and *Oh!* how we long to be among them!

No tunnel that narrows at the end to a
black door with only nothingness beyond

No shriek of tragic circumstances or event
however definitive and life-changing

No tsunami dark Punjabi swami however
fierce and calamitous with glowering eyebrows

can stop the love-beast in his tracks
or trap him in however velveteen a trap

But he moves on through thick and thin
touching with deft touch through
layer after layer the dormant heart
within

And each of us so touched displays a
curious fanning as of shutters of light and
dark almost falling open at that

astounding passage

And he smiles at himself in our own
faces that have now become mirrors for him to
smile in

And he laughs to himself at all our trembles and
bumbles and treble clef bawlings and bellows
until they all become reverberant

echoes of his laughter in an equally dazzling
hall of mirrors in which His Face alone
shows

And he is deft and svelte and swells to
enormous size though thinner than a
hair

And rushes like a river through our pulses
until our hearts are his reservoir

And we fall over falls in his barrel
and barely survive with only an

empty barrel to show for it while he alone
reaps all the glory

Since he is the love-beast and we aren't
even his whiskers or hooves but only the
tap tap tap of where he

deigns to come in so long as nothing else
is there to pen him in

Free in acting and desiring without the
least shred of action or desire

Free in longing and arriving without there being
anything in any future to long for or
arrive at

except the dissolution in pure explosion of all
longing and arriving as well as all future to
explode by his slightest chronological maneuver

as he pats our hearts in passing with a delicate
momentary feather-duster and
is gone
that sweet intangible
love-beast!

Who leaves us with only his
twin feet repeating those

delirious dance steps he took to
track us down

Gone now

Oh now
completely
gone!

9/30 (Rumi's 800th birthday)

COVERLETS

In life
blankets

In death
earth

10/2

MONUMENTALITY

The monumentality of even the tiniest living thing
makes those gnats flying around in here

God's co-pilots

The spirit of cornfields lies along the pillowed
divan of every cob of corn

adorned in silk

We won't mention each snowflake
most precious jewelry of nothingness who
gives emptiness razzle-dazzle for a
special moment from high space to earth
before being taken back by the Divine
Pawn Broker and put on His most secret
shelf

Things gone in an instant not unlike ourselves
like a charge of wild horses from point
A to point B along the edge of a
piece of paper upon which in rich
calligraphy is written only the
Divine Name (not even our own)
over and over and over again to the
full articulation of our living breaths

Ah the mountains The Himalayas the great piled

masses of rock and ice leaning against a
sky so blue turquoises fall up into it thinking
it's their mother

There Titans of respectability in monstrous
proportions aren't even a wink of bursting
bubble in the stretch of galaxies through a

hiccup of time

Though to us they've lived for millennia and will live so
further down the line

Though the line is only *There is no
God but Allah*

with the final *"h"* an outbreath reaching
to the End of Time

10/4

A FISH STORY

A fish swam up to the surface of a
lovely lake in Ceylon perhaps and

looked around

Those big round eyes took in what of the
world they could consume

and the picture assumed went straight to that
fish's heart since of brain a fish has so

very little

And he recognized at once that the
watery element he was in suited him

just fine

Yet a moose at the side of the lake
(so it must be Saskatchewan and not

Ceylon) caught a glimpse of this
sly and svelte swimmer and fell into a

huge antlered reverie of envy
thinking in its moosey brain

how lovely it would be to dive into the

deep and swim around

just at the moment a hunter admired it
through his camouflaged binoculars and

silently put them down and aimed his gun
whose *"pop!"* startled the fish back

down who thanked his Lord for a finer
frame in which to live just as he

spied a gangling worm aglitter in the
filtered sunlight and went to it with a

kind of *"why not"* flick of his dorsal

to which a sage rounding the mountain-bend
with staff and young boy at his side

said *"Both contentment and discontent
have their limits in this world*

*and only by holding to the King of this
world and the next will we*

*sense any relief and experience true
freedom from grief's*

elemental poundings"

10/5

LIQUID RUBIES

Liquid rubies bubble in the heart's crucible
into whose frothy brew crutches and crosses

collapsible stairways and blank doorways
opening on themselves but no passageway

churn and dissolve away
Because the heart is the place where dead men

never linger long nor haunt with their
blue faces the tree-lined esplanades there

since all are alive there nothing else
a crossroad place where the simplest thing

blesses rather than curses us

There's a house there
and in the upper floors reverberant echoes
of God calling Himself by His Holiest Names

mixed with canary song and wolf howl
hoot owl hoot and street brawl

but His Voice throughout it all calling
and calling because of His love for us

and some are caught in its sonorous net and saved

and some slip through the wide mesh and are
lost in the empty streets of their refusal to

listen

but everyone hears His call
even the criminal in his cell

and the bell before it is rung and the
song before it is sung to anyone or to

no one

I hear it and I want to run to the
edge of the world so as to hear nothing but

it alone
calling us home

10/5

THE AIRY TUNNELS OF ETERNITY

The saint's tomb resounds with an echo as if
inside the swirl of a conch shell

of higher dimensions contained within four walls
under pressure

a giant has set down next to a whirlwind
or just inside a waterfall slicing

rainbows out of its furious curtain of water
sprung into the air with their arc'd color spectrums

intact and shimmering

This place of endless repose and beginningless silence
where even a snail lowers its wet head

in reverence as it slides glisteningly by
its twin eyes retracted

O stand up inside this space to the
full length of your longing for God to

show His Face though he has
never refrained all the lights of your

days to do so
even to Robinson Crusoe

The saint smiles to himself in the
seclusion of his tomb which is life

letting all the white birds of the sky
fly free

through the airy tunnels of eternity

10/6

PARABLES FOR THE END OF RAMADAN

1

Once upon a time there was a tiny rabbit
not a runt of the litter not just the

last one chosen for the team nor the one
most likely to get lost in the lettuce patch

but a rabbit about the size of an ant
and full grown!

He hopped all right and his long ears
turned backward well enough to catch

sounds of approach and he did that
darling thing of standing up with forepaws

poised just so before scampering off
but he was truly minute

and his many brothers and sisters were
normal size with all the usual rabbity

variations of color while he was white as
a sheet of paper or perhaps because of his

size more like the ripped corner of a sheet of
paper

Well everyone from great grandpop down
had basically given him up for lost

a little bit of microscopic punctuation
in their run-on sentence of rabbit rabbit rabbit

rabbit rabbit rabbit rabbit rabbit
and then almost nothing and then

rabbit rabbit rabbit
but when the drought of ought eight hit and all the

wolves and foxes arrived hungrily out of
nowhere and ate all those rabbits

our dwarf rabbit continued to nibble undisturbed
with its spider friends and beetle buddies

and when the crisis was over one
beautiful Spring day he happened to

meet another very tiny rabbit of the
opposite gender and soon was a

proud papa to hundreds of tiny rabbits

So it goes to show that below the
usual threshold of human perception

lie phenomena as contented with
themselves being as they are as we in our

pride in our ability to open and close doors and
sit on chairs and talk about the

ills of the world we ourselves have
brought upon us

are

2

The poet was a parrot
and the parrot was a poet
though neither of them know it

The truck was a Turk and the
Turk was a truck
said the elephant's trunk

The circus was a curse
and the curse was a circus
said the attending nurses

3

The corner of the house sat dejected
far from all the other parts of the house

The fence also wondered to itself
why it couldn't commit to one side or the other

Doors had to convince themselves they were
doors whether open or shut

And stairways also felt compromised
whether going up or down

Where was any of this in a relative way?
How was anyone to be content?

The fireplace without a cozy crackle of flame
was a blackened hole in the wall

Windows really weren't anything except a
pane thinly distinguishing inside from outside

And of course everything accumulates dust
just as we will one day become dust fallen low

All this stillness was really movement
and all movement ended up as stillness

Space began to take notice of itself
containing all yet not itself being contained

Perspectives shifted and dimensions capsized
and time looked at its own watch and smiled

as rain fell in the garden like a
gentle percussion orchestra whose instruments

were everything it fell on
gently receiving its blessings

4

He keeps everything in order
his shirts on hangers trousers folded on
hanger bars just so with seams aligned

His desk neat drawers organized
bills paid debts repaid on time

Lawn in front kept neat tree in back
trimmed flowers watered and the
stones in place either side of his paths

his walk swept daily

though he has a rooster head with
comb flopped to one side prominent beak

and goat feet hooves aclittering as he walks

but a heart of pure silver and eyes that catch
light's every nuance dappling through the day

He awakes at dawn and sings his
heart out

heard across all the valleys
to the end of time

5

A down-pouring river of light falls into a field and keeps
pouring itself onto one particular spot

Flying Saucers are soon ruled out though it
seems no doubt to be a paranormal phenomena

No one dares get too near
People watch it pouring down from a goodly distance

This goes on for days
Farmer Pritchett can't drive his tractor there

Preachers prey on natural fears of sin and retribution
though the ray seems utterly benign a kind of

bright celestial geyser of dazzle that could become
one of the natural wonders of the world if it

only weren't so unnatural

A week went by and the light fell unabated
as life went on as usual

The mayor fiddled the books and became
richer by two million

Stan and Bess had their anticipated baby
Three horses foaled and goats procreated

day followed night and night day

The Miracle at Pritchett's Place it came
to be called

A month went by and still light poured down
though no one dared get too close

Then one day a butterfly flew into it
and came out a sorrel horse

No one saw it happen
but Pritchett had one more horse

and at that moment at the sound of
the new horse's whinny as it

cantered out on the dew-fresh field at dawn
an astonishing thing happened

The space at the west margin of the pouring
light began to unpeel or unveil itself outward

moving multi-dimensionally westward in a
counter-clockwise motion continuously

the light now pouring not in a small waterfall
but in an ever-widening curved curtain that

unfurled from that pivot point spherically across
the entire planetary globe until it had

swept completely around the earth and
linked up to the eastern margin of the original light-fall

at which moment it
ascended back to its Source

leaving everything transformed completely from what it was
not as you see it now but as it

inwardly is
bathed utterly in a godly

radiance each thing and being absolutely
enlightened in

itself and each thing
absolutely singing

10/7-10/12

OCTOBER 17

A snowman at the edge of the tundra
surveys his domain

as silhouette reindeer run along the far horizon
under a blue sun

Endless melting wastes to xylophones of cracks and
fissured screams in ice falsetto

And he thinks himself lucky *The Prince of
All He Surveys* as he also

melts away drip by
serene drip

and the reindeer continue galloping left to
right under a blue sun

here in my mind's eye or
heart's bathysphere

at bedside 5A.M.
Philadelphia Pennsylvania

October 17
2007

IN THE FACE OF DEATH

1

In the face of death you may want to
wrap everything in foil

or ride an elk
or sit among penguins

You may feel not much time has elapsed
since you first sat up

and too much time has passed
since that light-burst took you

But faced with the prospect of yours or
another's death or even just

being in the proximity (in this case our
cat of seventeen years having taken to sitting for

days under a table in the dark)

you might feel like taking to the air
or painting the door black

holding this notebook upside-down in a
well of song

or lying down next to a leopard
a tree fallen athwart the pathway

2

But this is all us on this side of it

lamenting the transformation

A train whistle seen but not heard

A flight of heron with no wings flapping

Fallen tree athwart the pathway

While on the other side is all
glory and consequence

calliopes in clouds and passageways past
every obstacle known to us

Before revelation we slaughtered pigs
ribboned a goat and sent it out

to absorb our crimes

Bled on paper or drew mustaches on dogs
turned around in this world to its

ultimate strangeness

The dead walk among us and
we walk among the dead

but our nakedness is their clothing
and their clothing our nakedness

Sinister spatiality made innocent again

River of forgetfulness and renewal

Solace above all to the lonesome heart

10/17-18

THE BIRD THAT SANG THAT LAST NOTE

The bird that sang that last note
Oh do it again!

The moment that took place between us
so lacily perfect *Repeat! Repeat!*

What were those words in their order
that so struck my heart?

But peaks go and leave neither
trace nor trap nor map to their

particular treasure
repeatable beyond measure

But in heart's innermost cave a spirit of them
lingers having invited all similar spirits

to sup on each eager reminder

God's Hall a vast reverberation chamber
where everything from Beowulf to the

end of time is recalled

O love put me there
at *that* table!

10/20

I PUT ON GLASSES

I put on glasses to clarify the visual world
and remember God to focus the life of light

Just as the leap of the rabbit to grant it
flight from its enemies

and the giraffe's neck to reach the
topmost leaves

and the doorsill and lintel
to pass from room to room

and the glittering dance of the
galaxies to keep us spinning

and the stars in our eyes to keep us
looking intently

and the small dot of light in the distance
to keep us facing forward

and the sudden stop in the midst of it all
to reflect on His Magnitude

And His Magnitude He has put on
to know Him

And His absence to increase our humanity
and His Presence to annihilate it

10/22

A LITTLE SQUARE

A little square becomes a garden

a little circle a dome

a triangle becomes a pyramid

a rectangle a book

10/24

IN THE FULLNESS OF TIME

In the fullness of time
when these rolling premonitious eyes
are sealed shut
and this mouth corked
the heart in its canopic jar of earth
endlessly rocking
feet facing west head east and
face like a flower furled
and the eagle flies slowly past casting
its cold eye
and the oceans rising

In the fullness of time when
velvet ceases to speak to its wearer
hair no longer falls over shoulders
buttons no longer go through their suitable slits
wheels cease to rotate
and no one's feet quite reach the pavement
and owls cry over vacant lots where
papers blow making that
blowing paper sound that wrinkles
space into time and time into
space and crickets
fiddle to no one

Where we go on because we must
with our loose sail hanging at the mast
into that volatile mist

making out the namesake of He Who has
made all this
each glint of pin in the air
each pin of air whose point stabbed through
nothingness makes every something stir
each anywhere

Earth a ball that rolls on its own in space
whose waters stick to it and thick clouds
cushion it
like a sunbeamed jewel heading endlessly
home in the
fullness of time
leaving us out of it

Oh God so far out of it after our
mortal involvement with it
strong-arming its ratchets and its gears
its circles and its squares
we always at the point of liftoff or the
point of pushed down
among its cypress lawns

In the simple fullness
with no time at all
when the sublime simply
takes over
and leaves this life blind and that one
fully sighted as if
for the first time

O shield us with Your Compassionate
stream

and wake us from this
rock salt dream of men and their fine

moan

and take us endlessly
home

10/28

OF COURSE

The cherry pickers stopped their cherry picking
and noticed little pianos suspended from
each leaf

The inspector of rodents pushed back the little
door expecting a mouse family and found
to his astonishment tiny people going about
their business in a tiny metropolis

A weary policeman answered a call and
knocked on a door to investigate but when
the door swung open he was in Timbuktu on a
camel in a bright red *djellaba* leading a
spice caravan

So these itinerant negative noises you
hear or hear about in this universe

may be way off the mark
things not being as bad as we think but in fact
simply quite different from what we think

with no expectations worth expecting behind
this leaf that door or those voices or
bright or dull-eyed faces
that we take for granted
when very saints may be driving that
taxi and of course angels hanging out that laundry of

white billowing bed sheets

Being of one substance with the Divine makes things both
much less and much more complicated than
at first glance

Since when the sea divided and made a safe pathway
the Jews expected to be drowned

and Job expected things to get
worse and worse which of course they did and
we might also

but radiance doesn't stop with blinding white light
as if a billion foil sheets were fluttering in sunlight

it's also in the softest smallest subtlest thing
at the same magnitude and on as
magnificent a scale

but contained in a smaller container
the way this poem keeps getting corners and edges
like a box full of pottery needing stiff sides to
protect its breakabilty from looseness

when in fact that area's been cleared of
all materiality from the very beginning for

God's pure smile to have a clear mirror to
reflect in and us His slivers of

reflected light to beam it all
back to Him

10/30

THE LICKING SEA

Sitting here
I see the sea like a great tongue

licking the earth
lick and lick and lick again

And the surf's foam soothes where the
licking makes lands' edges raw

And the earth is the same
undiminished

And the moon lathers it with whiteness

And a figure is lost in all this vision

And the sea licks the vision clean

the sea like a licking tongue

licks the vision clean

11/4

HEAD PRESSED AGAINST A PILLOW

With my head pressed against a pillow
I hear my heartbeat pulsing in my ear

and it's not a house falling down around its
foundations

nor cathedral bells calling shepherds in for
vespers

nor a black mountain rumbling in warning before
volcanic blast

and no flamingo flocks take off as one pink
flying cloud across a silver sky

no bison pound the plains to sheets of dust in a
galloping throb

nor oceans with all their graceful inhabitants
boom a message home

It's just one heart among many on a
pillow hillside past dusk

taking a nap before the evening
neither death encroaching nor the revels of

Venice behind half black and white masks

Neither a question nor an answer
across either a void or the fullness of light

though I do feel a kinship with a forest in the
dark with all her woodsy creatures either

finding their way to curl in sleep or
waking to hunt to a similar regular pulse as mine

of heartbeat heartbeat heartbeating
past both light and dark

who dictates this poem with its
ventricular mouth

God's Light
winding up and unwinding

tick by tick
to the sweetest

last quick drop

11/9

INDEX

ABOUT THE AUTHOR

Born in 1940 in Oakland, California, Daniel Abdal-Hayy Moore had his first book of poems, *Dawn Visions*, published by Lawrence Ferlinghetti of City Lights Books, San Francisco, in 1964, and the second in 1972, *Burnt Heart/Ode to the War Dead*. He created and directed *The Floating Lotus Magic Opera Company* in Berkeley, California in the late 60s, and presented two major productions, *The Walls Are Running Blood*, and *Bliss Apocalypse*. He became a Sufi Muslim in 1970, performed the Hajj in 1972, and lived and traveled throughout Morocco, Spain, Algeria and Nigeria, landing in California and publishing *The Desert is the Only Way Out*, and *Chronicles of Akhira* in the early 80s (Zilzal Press). Residing in Philadelphia since 1990, in 1996 he published *The Ramadan Sonnets* (Jusoor/City Lights), and in 2002, *The Blind Beekeeper* (Jusoor/ Syracuse University Press). He has been the major editor for a number of works, including *The Burdah* of Shaykh Busiri, translated by Hamza Yusuf, and the poetry of Palestinian poet, Mahmoud Darwish, translated by Munir Akash. He is also widely published on the worldwide web: *The American Muslim,* and his own website *www.ecstaticxchange.com*. He has been poetry editor for *Seasons Journal, Islamica Magazine,* a 2010 translation by Munir Akash of *State of Siege,* by Mahmoud Darwish (Syracuse University Press), and *The Prayer of the Oppressed*, by Imam Muhammad Nasir al-Dar'i, translated by Hamza Yusuf. In 2011, 2012 and 2014 he was a winner of the Nazim Hikmet Prize for Poetry. In 2013 he won an American Book Award, and in 2013 and 2014 was listed among The 500 Most Influential Muslims for his poetry. *The Ecstatic Exchange Series* is bringing out the extensive body of his works of poetry (a complete list of published works on page 2).

POETIC WORKS by Daniel Abdal-Hayy Moore
Published and Unpublished

Dawn Visions (published by City Lights, 1964)
Burnt Heart/Ode to the War Dead (published by City Lights, 1972)
This Body of Black Light Gone Through the Diamond (printed by Fred
    Stone, Cambridge, Mass, 1965)
On The Streets at Night Alone (1965?)
All Hail the Surgical Lamp (1967)
States of Amazement (1970)

Abdallah Jones and the Disappearing-Dust Caper (published by The
    Ecstatic Exchange/Crescent Series, 2006)
'Ala ud-Deen and the Magic Lamp (published by The Ecstatic Exchange, 2011)
The Chronicles of Akhira (1981) (published by Zilzal Press with
    Typoglyphs by Karl Kempton, 1986; published in Sparrow on the
    Prophet's Tomb by The Ecstatic Exchange, 2009)
Mouloud (1984) (A Zilzal Press chapbook, 1995; published in Sparrow on
    the Prophet's Tomb by The Ecstatic Exchange, 2009)
The Crown of Creation (1984) (published by The Ecstatic Exchange, 2012)
The Look of the Lion (The Parabolas of Sight) (1984)
The Desert is the Only Way Out (completed 4/21/84) (Zilzal Press chapbook,
    1985)
Atomic Dance (1984) (am here books, 1988)
Outlandish Tales (1984)
Awake as Never Before (12/26/84) (Zilzal Press chapbook, 1993)
Glorious Intervals (1/1/85) (Zilzal Press chapbook, ?)
Long Days on Earth/Book I (1/28 – 8/30/85)
Long Days on Earth/Book II (Hayy Ibn Yaqzan)
Long Days on Earth/Book III (1/22/86)
Long Days on Earth/Book IV (1986)
The Ramadan Sonnets (Long Days on Earth/Book V) (5/9 – 6/11/86)
    (published by Jusoor/City Lights Books, 1996) (republished as Ramadan
    Sonnets by The Ecstatic Exchange, 2005)
Long Days on Earth/Book VI (6-8/30/86)
Holograms (9/4/86 – 3/26/87)
History of the World (The Epic of Man's Survival) (4/7 – 6/18/87)
Exploratory Odes (6/25 – 10/18/87)

The Man at the End of the World (11/11 – 12/10/87)

The Perfect Orchestra (3/30 – 7/25/88)(published by The Ecstatic Exchange, 2009)

Fed from Underground Springs (7/30 – 11/23/88)

Ideas of the Heart (11/27/88 – 5/5/89)

New Poems (scattered poems, out of series, from 3/24 – 8/9/89)

Facing Mecca (5/16 – 11/11/89) (published by The Ecstatic Exchange, 2014)

A Maddening Disregard for the Passage of Time (11/17/89 – 5/20/90) (published by The Ecstatic Exchange, 2009)

The Heart Falls in Love with Visions of Perfection (6/15/90 – 6/2/91)

Like When You Wave at a Train and the Train Hoots Back at You (Farid's Book) (6/11 – 7/26/91) (published by The Ecstatic Exchange, 2008)

Orpheus Meets Morpheus (8/1/91– 3/14/92)

The Puzzle (3/21/92 – 8/17/93)(published by The Ecstatic Exchange, 2011)

The Greater Vehicle (10/17/93 – 4/30/94)

A Hundred Little 3-D Pictures (5/14/94 – 9/11/95) (published by The Estatic Exchange, 2013)

The Angel Broadcast (9/29 – 12/17/95)

Mecca/Medina Time-Warp (12/19/95 – 1/6/96) (published as a Zilzal Press chapbook, 1996)(published in Sparrow on the Prophet's Tomb, 2009)

Miracle Songs for the Millennium (1/20 – 10/16/96)(published by The Ecstatic Exchange, 2014)

The Blind Beekeeper (11/15/96 – 5/30/97) (published 2002 by Jusoor/ Syracuse University Press)

Chants for the Beauty Feast (6/3 – 10/28/97)(published by The Ecstatic Exchange, 2011

You Open a Door and it's a Starry Night (10/29/97 – 5/23/98) (published by The Ecstatic Exchange, 2009)

Salt Prayers (5/29 – 10/24/98) (published by The Ecstatic Exchange, 2005)

Some (10/25/98 – 4/25/99) (published by The Ecstatic Exchange, 2014)

Flight to Egypt (5/1 – 5/16/99)

I Imagine a Lion (5/21 – 11/15/99) (published by The Ecstatic Exchange, 2006)

Millennial Prognostications (11/25/99 – 2/2/2000) (published by the Ecstatic Exchange, 2009)

Shaking the Quicksilver Pool (2/4 – 10/8/2000) (published by The Ecstatic Exchange, 2009)

Blood Songs (10/9/2000 – 4/3/2001)(Published by The Ecstatic Exchange, 2012)

The Music Space (4/10 – 9/16/2001) (published by The Ecstatic Exchange, 2007)

Where Death Goes (9/20/2001 – 5/1/2002) (published by The Ecstatic Exchange, 2009)

The Flame of Transformation Turns to Light (99 Ghazals Written in English) (5/14 – 8/21/2002) (published by The Ecstatic Exchange, 2007)

Through Rose-Colored Glasses (7/22/2002 – 1/15/2003) (published by The Ecstatic Exchange, 2007)

Psalms for the Broken-Hearted (1/22 – 5/25/2003) (published by The Ecstatic Exchange, 2006)

Hoopoe's Argument (5/27 – 9/18/03)

Love is a Letter Burning in a High Wind (9/21 – 11/6/2003) (published by The Ecstatic Exchange, 2006)

Laughing Buddha/Weeping Sufi (11/7/2003 – 1/10/2004) (published by The Ecstatic Exchange, 2005)

Mars and Beyond (1/20 – 3/29/2004) (published by The Ecstatic Exchange, 2005)

Underwater Galaxies (4/5 – 7/21/2004) (published by The Ecstatic Exchange, 2007)

Cooked Oranges (7/23/2004 – 1/24/2005 (published by The Ecstatic Exchange, 2007)

Holiday from the Perfect Crime (1/25 – 6/11/2005) (published by The Ecstatic Exchange, 2011)

Stories Too Fiery to Sing Too Watery to Whisper (6/13 – 10/24/2005) (published by The Ecstatic Exchange, 2014)

Coattails of the Saint (10/26/2005 – 5/10/2006) (published by The Ecstatic Exchange, 2006)

In the Realm of Neither (5/14/2006 – 11/12/06) (published by The Ecstatic Exchange, 2008)

Invention of the Wheel (11/13/06 – 6/10/07)(published by The Ecstatic Exchange, 2010)

The Sound of Geese Over the House (6/15 – 11/4/07)(published by The Ecstatic Exchange, 2015)

The Fire Eater's Lunchbreak (11/11/07 – 5/19/2008) (published by The Ecstatic Exchange, 2008)

Sparks Off the Main Strike (5/24/2008 – 1/10/2009)(published by The Ecstatic Exchange, 2010)

Stretched Out on Amethysts (1/13 – 9/17/2009)(published by The Ecstatic Exchange, 2010)

The Throne Perpendicular to All that is Horizontal (9/18/09 – 1/25/10) (published by The Ecstatic Exchange, 2014)

In Constant Incandescence (2/10 – 8/13/10) (published by The Ecstatic Exchange, 2011)

The Caged Bear Spies the Angel (8/30/10 – 3/6/11)(published by The Ecstatic Exchange, 2010)

This Light Slants Upward (3/7 – 10/13/11)

Ramadan is Burnished Sunlight (part of This Light Slants Upward, published separately by The Ecstatic Exchange, 2011)

The Match That Becomes a Conflagration (10/14/11 – 5/9/12)

Down at the Deep End (5/10 – 8/3/12) (published by The Ecstatic Exchange, 2012)

Next Life (8/9/12 – 2/12/13) (published by The Ecstatic Exchange, 2013)

The Soul's Home (2/13 – 10/8/13) (published by The Ecstatic Exchange, 2014)

Eternity Shimmers & Time Holds its Breath (10/10/13 – 1/27/14) (published by The Ecstatic Exchange, 2014)

He Comes Running (part of Eternity Shimmers, published as an Ecstatic Exchange Chapbook, 2014)

The Sweet Enigma of it All (1/29 – 6/18/14) (published by The Ecstatic Exchange, 2014)

Let Me See Diamonds Everywhere I Look (6/18/14 – 1/15/15)

With Every Breath (1/18/15 --)

White Noise in This World Silver in the Next (5/1/15 --)

www.ingramcontent.com/pod-product-compliance
Lightning Source LLC
Chambersburg PA
CBHW030712110426
R18122000003B/R181220PG42736CBX00012B/11